Made in the USA
Las Vegas, NV
20 May 2022

49111821R00070